Types of Volcanoes

by Julie Murray

Level 1 – Beginning
Short and simple sentences with familiar words or patterns for children who are beginning to understand how letters and sounds go together.

Level 2 – Emerging
Longer words and sentences with more complex language patterns for readers who are practicing common words and letter sounds.

Level 3 – Transitional
More developed language and vocabulary for readers who are becoming more independent.

abdobooks.com

Published by Abdo Zoom, a division of ABDO, PO Box 398166, Minneapolis, Minnesota 55439. Copyright © 2023 by Abdo Consulting Group, Inc. International copyrights reserved in all countries. No part of this book may be reproduced in any form without written permission from the publisher. Dash!™ is a trademark and logo of Abdo Zoom.

Printed in the United States of America, North Mankato, Minnesota.
052022
092022

Photo Credits: Alamy, Getty Images, Shutterstock
Production Contributors: Kenny Abdo, Jennie Forsberg, Grace Hansen, John Hansen
Design Contributors: Candice Keimig, Neil Klinepier

Library of Congress Control Number: 2021950304

Publisher's Cataloging in Publication Data

Names: Murray, Julie, author.
Title: Types of volcanoes / by Julie Murray.
Description: Minneapolis, Minnesota : Abdo Zoom, 2023 | Series: Volcano science | Includes online resources and index.
Identifiers: ISBN 9781098228408 (lib. bdg.) | ISBN 9781098229245 (ebook) | ISBN 9781098229665 (Read-to-Me ebook)
Subjects: LCSH: Volcanoes--Juvenile literature. | Volcanic eruptions--Juvenile literature. | Volcanism--Juvenile literature. | Physical geography--Juvenile literature.
Classification: DDC 551.21--dc23

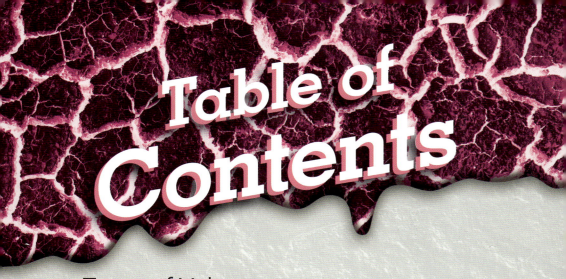

Table of Contents

Types of Volcanoes 4

Shield and Composite Volcanoes. 8

Lava Domes and Cinder Cones 16

The State of a Volcano. 22

Glossary 23

Index 24

Online Resources 24

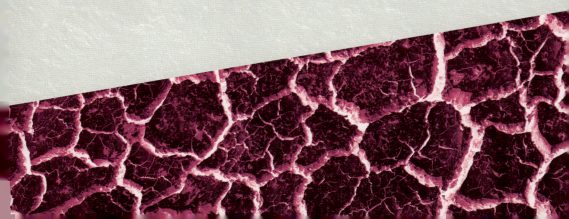

Types of Volcanoes

There are four types of volcanoes. They are shield volcanoes, composite volcanoes, lava domes, and cinder cones.

Shield Volcano

Composite Volcano

Lava Dome

Cinder Cone

A volcano is grouped by its shape. A volcano's shape tells how it was formed. It also indicates what type of eruption it will produce.

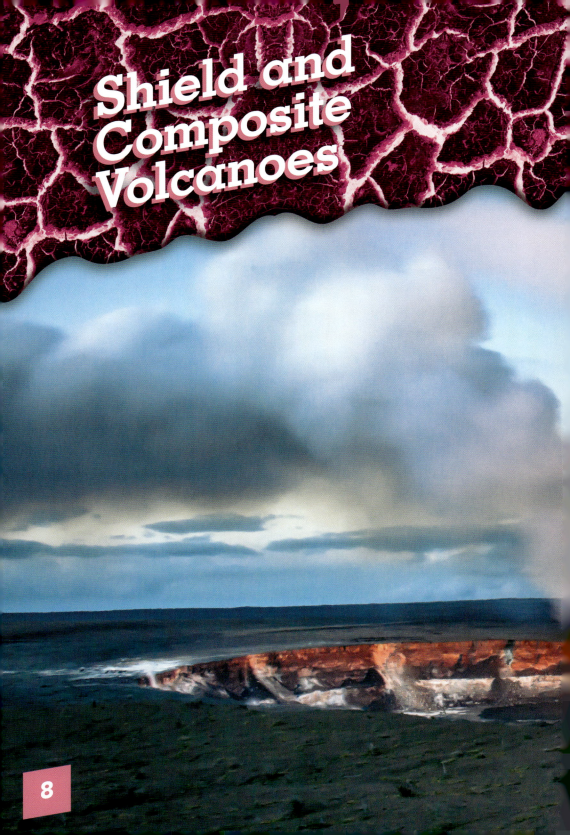

Shield and Composite Volcanoes

8

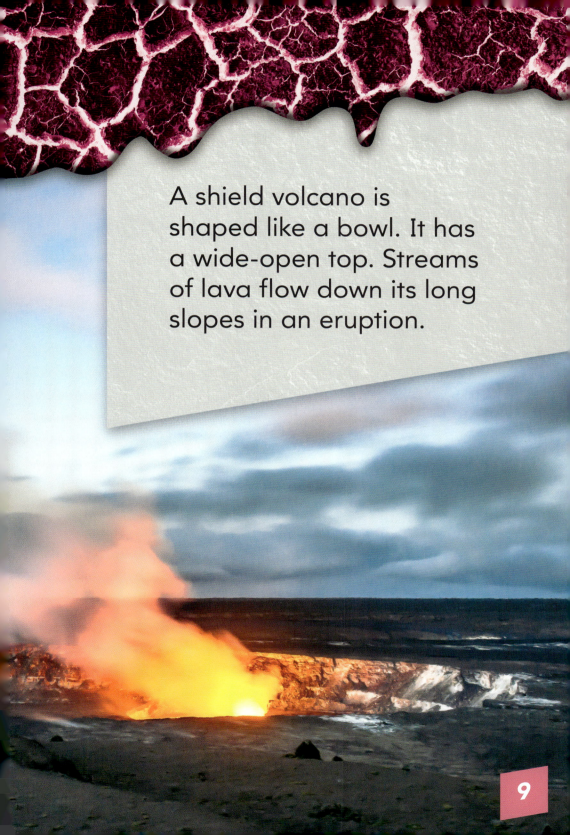

A shield volcano is shaped like a bowl. It has a wide-open top. Streams of lava flow down its long slopes in an eruption.

After an eruption, the lava hardens and the volcano grows bigger. Shield volcanoes erupt often and for long periods of time.

A composite volcano has **steep** sides. It is made up of many layers of **volcanic rock**.

13

Thick magma traps gases, building **pressure** in the magma chamber. When a composite volcano finally erupts, it sends out huge clouds of burning rocks and gas.

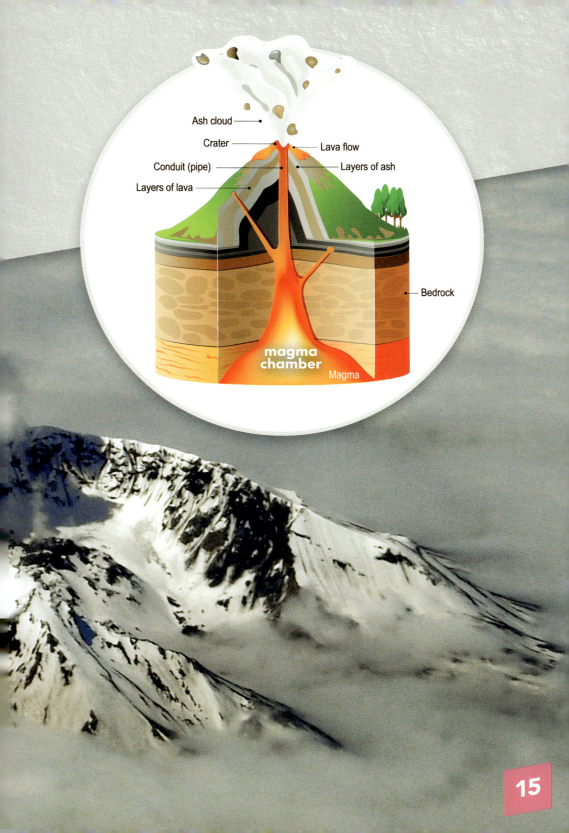

Lava Domes and Cinder Cones

A lava dome forms near a volcanic **vent**. Lava builds up and forms a dome shape. Lava domes can erupt or **collapse** over time. They are often found inside composite volcanoes.

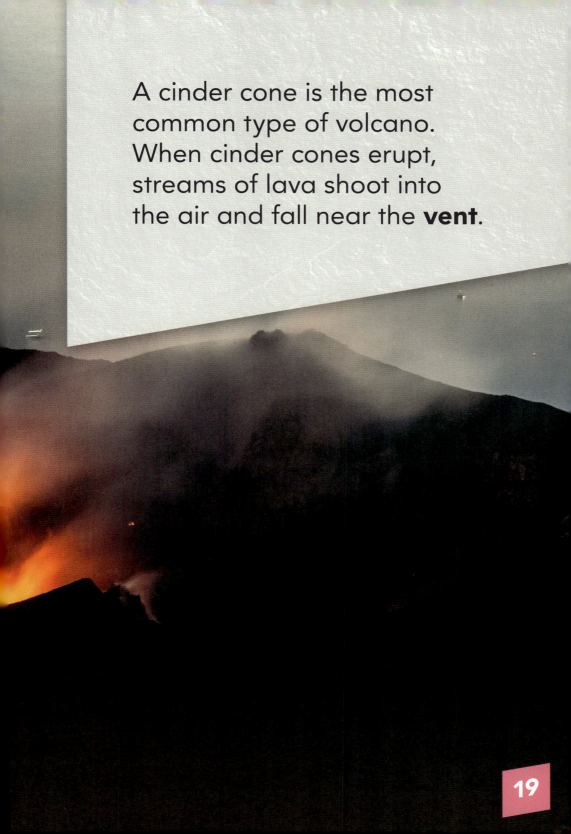

A cinder cone is the most common type of volcano. When cinder cones erupt, streams of lava shoot into the air and fall near the **vent**.

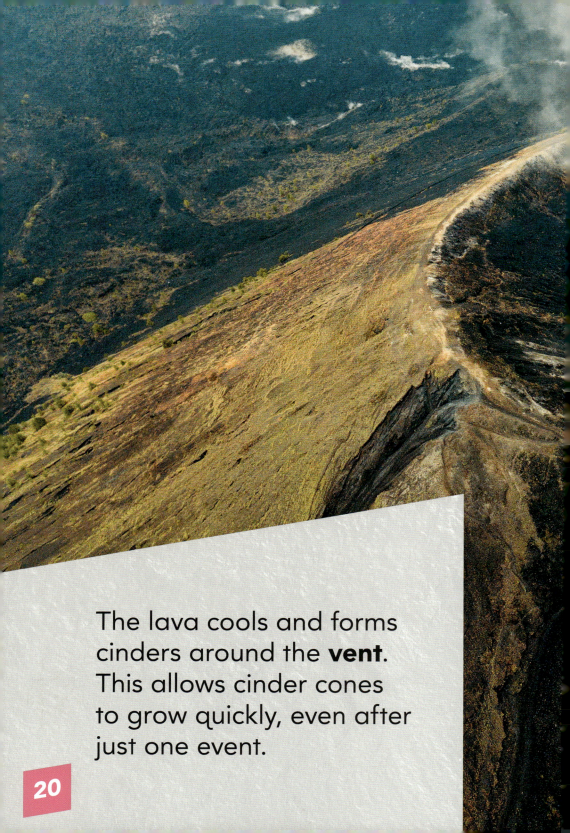

The lava cools and forms cinders around the **vent**. This allows cinder cones to grow quickly, even after just one event.

The State of a Volcano

- **Active** – a volcano that has recently erupted and is likely to erupt in the future

- **Dormant** – a volcano that has not erupted for a very long time but may erupt in the future

- **Erupting** – an active volcano that is currently having an eruption

- **Extinct** – has not erupted for more than 10,000 years and is unlikely to erupt in the future because the magma supply has been cut off

Glossary

collapse – to fall down, give way, or cave in.

pressure – a steady force upon a surface.

steep – having a sharp slope or slant.

vent – an opening through which a gas or vapor can pass through.

volcanic rock – a rock formed by lava.

Index

cinder cone 4, 19, 20

composite volcano 4, 13, 14, 17

gases 14

lava 9, 10, 17, 19, 20

lava dome 4, 17

magma 14

shield volcano 4, 9, 10

Online Resources

Booklinks NONFICTION NETWORK
FREE! ONLINE NONFICTION RESOURCES

To learn more about types of volcanoes, please visit **abdobooklinks.com** or scan this QR code. These links are routinely monitored and updated to provide the most current information available.